33 Ways to Work with Your Dreams

A Beginner's Guide to Dream Work

PAMELA MULLER

DEDICATION

Dreams are sacred things, and sharing a dream is a brave and daring act of vulnerability. This book is dedicated to my inner circle of dreamers: Those who have shown up for dream groups, retreats, parties, and one-on-one's, and all who have shared a dream with me. This collection is for you.

ACKNOWLEDGMENTS

Thank you Brett, Matthew, Mom, Anthony, Barbara, Bonnie, and Dad.
I love you.

Pamela Muller

"You have a story to tell. I promise your dreams are helping you tell it. All you have to do is learn to listen."

Introduction

Welcome, sweet reader, to what I hope will become your favorite little dream book, *33 Ways to Work with Your Dreams: A Beginner's Guide to Dream Work.*

In these pages, I share 33 different strategies you can use to unpack your dreams and discover their meaning. I am Sweet Georgia Pam, a trained spiritual director and dream expert. I have more than a decade of experience in this work and a lifetime of passion for dreams.

My own journey through life, with its various crises and celebrations, taught me the value of being able to discern the wisdom that comes from my nighttime dreams.

Before working with my dreams, I lived my life listening to everyone else's wisdom. I made my choices based on other people's advice. But after becoming aware of my dreams' capacity to tell me the truth about myself, I began to seek my own inner counsel.

Learning to work with my dreams helped me approach the things I feared most in life with more confidence, and taught me how to own my decisions and choices.

Dreams were most helpful for me when I needed to distinguish my own inner voice from the voices in the outside world. Learning to work with my dreams helped me see myself more honestly and to recognize that my inner voice was, in fact guiding me all along.

That is what I want for you. I want you to use this book to dialogue with your dreaming mind and to come to trust that she is showing you the truth about yourself. You'll learn that dreams have the capacity to show you things that may be difficult for you to face, but in a way that allows for gentle self-reflection. You'll learn how to be honest with yourself.

Your dreams exist to help you. They tell the rest of your story—the part that you have not owned up to or lived into yet. When you unpack a dream using the strategies in this book, you'll find great wisdom contained within, wisdom specifically created from your life experiences. It only takes a little learning to begin to understand the language of your inner voice, and this book is a perfect starting place.

About Dreams and Dream Work

Dreams are complex picture metaphors representing your life and they are layered with meaning. They are not impossible to understand, even though it sometimes seems that way.

Dream work is the process of exploring the symbols and actions in a dream to extract some new, meaningful insight for your life. Dream work is not an exact science. It is a creative, intuitive process. It's an art form that takes practice. Luckily, we dream nearly every night, so there is plenty of material to practice with.

Good dream work creatively explores many different ideas about a dream's meaning and then pays attention, and listens intuitively, to your body's reaction to that exploration.

My approach is based on years of experience in the field of dreams, training in the Haden Institute's model of dream work, and Carl Jung's ideas about the psychology of dreams. In his work, Jung explains that when exploring a dream's meaning, the dreamer will feel a certain "Aha!" moment when some new and significant association is made between the dream and the dreamer's waking life. This deep resonance signals that you're on the right track to understand what the dream has come to tell you.

The more dreams you practice with, the more familiar you will become with your own "Aha!" reaction. This is your inner compass alerting you that what you're exploring feels right. Record those moments of resonance, those "Aha!" moments, and know that your inner voice is speaking to you in those moments, telling you to pay attention.

Once you make a connection between some waking life situation and a dream, then you can explore what the dream might be trying to help you see or understand. Dreams offer us the rest of the story and give us an opportunity for a different view or a new depth of understanding and empathy.

Dream work is the art of unpacking the experience of a dream and learning why it was created. My ultimate line of questioning when working with a dream goes something like this: "What waking life experiences did my dreaming mind choose to build a dream around and why was that waking life experience chosen?" When I explore all the ways to work with the dream and finally settle on some major "Aha!" between waking life and the dream, then I might ask myself, "When I combine the experience of this dream with the experience of the waking life situation, what new information is revealed to me?"

The more you work your dreams, the more familiar the process will feel to you and the more confident you will become in dream work.

This collection of ideas is meant to give you the tools you need to get started on a wonderful journey of self-discovery, a broad net to cast over each dream to try and capture its essence.

Use the ideas here to look creatively and playfully at your dreams. Each technique can be used on its own or in combination with one or more of the others. They are not meant to be followed in order. You are free to jump around. You'll likely find that some dreams lend themselves more naturally to one technique over the others.

As you read through these pages and put these strategies into practice, pay attention to what dreams show up in the coming nights and then work them while listening for that intuitive nudge that lets you know you've discovered something new.

Good luck and sweet dreaming,

#1 Write Down Your Dreams

Whether you call yourself a nondreamer or a vivid dreamer, writing down your dreams when you have them will help you. For nondreamers, planning to write something each morning when you wake up can trigger you to remember a dream. You are actually dreaming nearly every night when you sleep, you're just not remembering them. By planning to write down the next dream you have, you're more likely to remember one.

If you're a vivid dreamer, it's likely that you receive an onslaught of dreams night after night. For you, writing down a dream helps to slow down that mental activity a bit.

Writing out a dream also serves the purpose of making you decide which dreams are important enough to take the time to write down. If you want to start today, but don't remember a recent dream, go ahead and revisit one from your past. Writing a dream from months (or years) ago is still fruitful work. as your dreams do not expire.

If you are not fond of writing or you consider writing too laborious, then telling the dream out loud will also work. Whether you record it on paper or verbally will not matter as much as *that* you record it. It is the act of writing down or speaking a dream out loud that will help you begin to listen to your dreams.

(#2) Title Your Dreams

Giving each dream a title helps you quickly identify important components of the dream. It also helps during those mornings when you don't have the time to write down the entire dream. The title can satisfy the need to record at least some part of a dream. Jotting down the date and title of your dream can act as a holding place until you can journal more completely.

When a dream is long and detailed or when it jumps around wildly between scenes and storylines, finding the right title can be a challenge. Do not concern yourself with coming up with the perfect title right away. I find that sometimes a simple title will suffice at first. And then, after I have worked the dream using some other strategies and become familiar with its essence, I might go back and change the title to something that feels more accurate.

You might start keeping a simple log of dates and dream titles in the front of your journal. It makes a great reference for revisiting important dreams.

#3 Make Waking Life Associations

Looking at a dream and asking the simple question, "What does this remind me of in my waking life?" might uncover clues about a dream's meaning. Making waking life associations means looking for any link between an event you encountered in waking life and the dream (or dream symbol).

As you write or recount the dream, consider what it reminds you of from your waking life. It can be anything that might be connected to this dream in any way. The color in the dream reminds you of the color of your boss's car, or the way a certain character behaved in the dream reminds you a little bit of your favorite singer.

Some waking life associations are crystal clear and pop up instantly in your mind, while others take some time to arise. For that reason, you should take your time with this strategy and be sure to write down any and all ideas that come to mind. Do not dismiss any similarities. Remember, the goal of dream work is to amass a brainstorm of thoughts and then sift through them for the ones that seem most strongly associated with the dream.

Once you connect something from the dream with something from waking life, then you can move into exploring what commentary the dream is making about that waking life situation.

#4 Use Dream Dictionaries

A dream dictionary is a reference book that interprets specific symbols. There are countless dream dictionaries available online and in bookstores.

Dream dictionaries can teach you how metaphors and symbols have been interpreted over time and across cultures. And that can open up new ways of understanding your dreams.

When consulting a dream dictionary, you only need to look up what you consider to be the main symbols from a dream. That means you have to decide what images or actions in the dream are considered the "main" ones. Doing that is helpful in and of itself. Then, when you look up the main symbol(s), you'll find a definition of the meaning.

Dream dictionaries help you begin to consider various ways to think about each symbol. But please do not take what is written as definitive and stop there. The usefulness of dream dictionaries is due to the sheer variety of ideas they offer. They may reference certain cultural, historical, societal, or mythical associations you would not have otherwise considered.

#5 Define a Symbol for Yourself

After you look through a few different symbol interpretations from other resources, give it a try yourself. Think about your own personal experiences with the symbols in your dream.

For example, if a bear appears in your dream, you might ask yourself questions like these:

- What do I think of bears?
- How do I feel about them?
- Do I have any specific fears concerning bears?
- What are my personal experiences (if any) with bears?
- Do I know of any familiar stories or movies that contain a bear? If so, what did the bear mean in the story?
- Have I encountered any animals similar to a bear in waking life recently?

In essence, you're defining the dream symbol(s) based on your own personal associations, based on your own interpretation. When I first started doing dream work, I did not trust my own associations. I thought the dictionaries knew more than I did about dream symbolism, and while I was still learning to think and speak in that symbolic way, they did. The dictionaries showed me how to think symbolically. But my own associations were always just as valid as the ones from other "expert" resources. I want you to learn to trust your own interpretations. Begin by defining a symbol for yourself, and then see how closely it matches what you find in your dream research.

#6 Sit with the Tension

Ask yourself: "Where is the tension highest in this dream?" or "Where is the energy the greatest?"

Identify the moment of tension in the dream, and then spend time envisioning it. In your mind's eye, sit inside this part of the dream for as long as you can. Just see what you notice.

By observing and sitting with the tension in a dream, your gentle curiosity makes space around the scene. And in the same way that sitting in a yoga pose for several minutes deepens your pose, sitting inside the tension of a dream may deepen your experience of it.

This type of contemplative dream work can trigger surprising responses, such as a sudden wave of emotion, an abrupt waking life association that seems to come out of nowhere, or a distant memory directly connected to the dream. All these realizations are natural reminders that contemplation can lead to profound insights.

It is important to note that not all dreams will have an obvious point of tension or heightened energy. For these dreams, choose a part of the dream you want to know more about and focus on it with the same curious gaze.

#7 Get Better Sleep

Sleep is obviously a part of the dreaming process, but what may not be so obvious is that improving the quality of your sleep can enhance the work you do with your dreams.

Because dreams are a natural phenomenon and an activity that happens while your body is sleeping, it stands to reason that the healthier your sleep habits are the more natural and healthy your dreams will be.

A workshop attendee once shared with me that he used to have horrible nightmares every night until he went to a sleep specialist who informed him that he had severe sleep apnea (a common sleep disorder). He followed his doctor's orders and began sleeping peacefully. "After that," he told me, "my dreams returned to normal and I could finally enjoy dreaming." This may or may not apply to you. I am merely pointing out the healthier your sleep habits, the more likely you are to have a "normal" relationship with your dreams.

You might find that by putting a little more emphasis on the quality of your sleep, you'll be rewarded with more memorable and workable dreams.

#8 Understand Characters as Qualities

People dream of their friends, family, lovers, and enemies all the time. A known person in your dream is often a stand-in for those qualities you associate with him or her.

Identifying the qualities you connect with that person can give you new insights into ways you might need to incorporate that person's personality or character traits into your waking life.

When working a dream with a familiar person in it, I will sometimes ask the dreamer, "Tell me about that person. How would you describe him or her?" Then we explore how the descriptions might apply to waking life situations. I want to emphasize that this is not an investigation into that person, but into what that person may represent in your dreaming life. This usually leads to an insight about how that person in waking life is acting as your teacher at the moment.

For example, people often dream of an ex-lover and then come to me fearing that it means they are not happy in their current relationship. Once we refocus on the ex-lover as a set of character traits, rather than an actual person, it usually changes the discussion from fear (or longing) to curiosity. "What does this mean about my ex?" turns into "What might I be needing or wanting right now that relates to my relationship with that person?"

Identifying what each character represents helps you stay focused on your development.

#9 Continue the Conversation

Getting into dialogue with characters who show up in your dreams can help you get more information out of them. It takes some practice if you're not used to creative writing or stream-of-consciousness journaling, but if you are willing to try, it can pay off with powerful insights.

This strategy assumes that all characters in your dream are aspects of yourself. They are different expressions of your own psyche. If that is assumed, then having a conversation with a part of yourself may reveal some perspective or information that isn't yet conscious to you.

To do this, first consider what you'd like to know from this character. Maybe you wonder why he came or maybe you want to know how to make her behave differently. Review the dream in your mind and decide what question(s) you'd like to ask.

Then break out your journal and try writing the story of that conversation. Don't worry if this feels awkward. Be open to whatever ideas come to you as you write.

#10 Spend a Week with an Image

Spending a week with a dream image is a great way to open up to new insights about what it means for you. It's a way to let the image from a dream integrate more deeply into your waking world.

Choose a dream image that carries a lot of energy. Dreams are full of charged images, so choosing just one might be a challenge. Start with a recent or recurring image.

Hold that image in your mind and focus on it as you go about your waking life. Notice where/when that image comes to mind during the week. Journal about what you find and review it at the end of the week.

The goal of this exercise is not to come to a full understanding of the image's place in your dream and in your waking life, but to appreciate the depth of the image and its connection to you.

Dreams, and the images in them, are much more layered, complex, and wise than we imagine. This technique invites you to experience the breadth of what's available to you through dream work.

#11 List the Emotions

Listing the emotions you felt in a dream can sometimes shed light on a connection you didn't know was there.

On a sheet of paper, list the emotions as they occurred in your dream. When doing this exercise, don't settle for the first word that comes to mind. Take time to choose the right words to describe your emotional state. For example, maybe the word *scared* comes to mind first, but isn't quite the emotion you felt. Maybe you were more *concerned* than scared. Or maybe concerned and scared sort of describe it, but when you really put yourself back inside the dream, you realize you were actually feeling *apprehensive*. Search for the word that most accurately describes the way you felt in the dream. The more thoroughly descriptive your list, the better.

Look at the list as a single series of emotions in the order they are written. When you do this, you might find that a similar waking life situation is creating that same movement of emotions. This can help you skip the analogy of symbols and go straight to the heart of the dream's purpose.

This works better for some dreams than for others. Some dreams are mundane and lacking in strong emotional content. That will make it difficult to notice anything. But for those dreams that are vivid in their emotional experience, this strategy can help you cut through the confusion.

#12 Identify Repeating Symbols

Dream symbols like to repeat themselves. Noticing similar symbols across different dreams can help you connect with the meaning between dreams. Often, a symbol will show up over and over while you are wrestling with a specific life issue and then will disappear when that life issue is resolved.

Keeping a dream journal helps you spot similarities among dreams, as does paying attention and thinking back through any dreams you recall from your past. However you track them, identifying a repeating dream symbol and figuring out what it represents gives you a starting place when it shows up in future dreams.

I have one client who frequently dreams of babies she is responsible for, but who are not her own children. The children vary, and the circumstances surrounding them vary, but one thing is the same. In her dreams, she is responsible for them and they are not hers. In working the symbol, she discovered that when this situation shows up in dreams, no matter the variation, it means that she has taken on some responsibility in waking life that does not belong to her. Knowing this helps her address the issue in waking life as soon as it arises in her dream life.

#13 Group Dreams by Time Frame

Because dreams are often connected to issues you are concerned with in waking life, it's useful to look at a group of dreams that comes from a certain chapter of your life and notice what, if anything, connects them.

Take a series of dreams from a chapter in your life that you want to explore and write out each dream. Then scan all of them together for similarities. Maybe they all have a certain character, or perhaps the mood of the dream is the same. Maybe they all have water in them, or the main character is running in the dreams. They won't all be mirror images of each other, but you may pick up on a pattern flowing through the dream series.

The links between dreams suggest how they express the evolution of a situation in waking life. For example, maybe the water in your dreams slowly becomes more calm and clear as an emotional waking life situation resolves itself.

Dreams that show up within a few days of each other are perfect for this strategy. The next time you experience two or more dreams in a short time frame, capture them in writing and see how they may be working together.

#14 Pay Attention to Color

Color is representative of our preverbal association to emotions. Color does not always play a significant role in dreams. But when it does, it's worth exploring that component.

Color is used in advertisements as a means to influence us on an unconscious level. So it stands to reason that our unconscious mental activity (i.e., the dreaming mind) might also employ the use of color as a means of influence.

As with all dream symbols, it is important to begin with your own personal associations to the color before referring to outside resources (dream dictionaries, professionals, or scientific research about human associations to color, e.g.).

You might ask questions like, "Where have I seen this specific color recently?" or "What does this color remind me of?" Is there something in your past that you associate with this color? If so, it may mean that past situation has something to offer you today.

(#15) Use Your Imagination

Sometimes the best way to get new insights from a dream is to use your imagination. Reenter the dream in your mind and do whatever you want. Just roam around inside the dream for a few minutes and notice what happens. Notice how the dream shifts, seemingly on its own, in response to your exploration and participation.

Dreams take place in that imaginative realm, so going into the landscape of a dream while you're awake will allow you to coexist in that realm as both conscious thought (i.e., imagination) and unconscious response (i.e., automatic reaction to your efforts).

I suggest that you try this in a quiet place, seated or lying down. Keep your journal handy to record any thoughts that come to you during this activity.

#16 Make a Timeline

Recurring dreams are dreams we have again and again. They are usually negative dreams that are triggered by waking life stress. Recurring dreams are like a habit your mind has picked up in response to a set of emotions.

In order to unpack a recurring dream, think about all of the instances of the dream you can recall. Go back as far as you can remember having the dream. Ask yourself, when was the first time you recall having the dream and what was happening in your life at that time. See if you can link that type of experience to other times when you had the dream.

For example, if someone has a particularly bad relationship with a spouse and then divorces from him or her, they may have a dream that encapsulates their negative experience with that person. Later, when a new person enters their life who is similar or who calls up a similar emotional response as the ex, they might have a recurring dream. This is the mind's attempt to learn from past mistakes and remind the dreamer of potential pitfalls with the new relationship.

A timeline may help you connect your recurring dream to some significant life pattern.

#17 Describe the Weirdest Part

Sometimes the strangest things in a dream are key to understanding its message. Ask yourself, "What was the *naked parade* weirdest part of my dream?" Maybe there is a detail that *pp* seems to jump out as the most bizarre. That attribute is *gay 20 Hs rs* telling you something specific, and if you can connect it to waking life, it may unlock the rest of the puzzle. Find that nugget and then try to describe it in as many ways as you can. See if any of it sounds familiar to your waking life.

For example, in one of my dreams there was a deep pool of water in the middle of the woods. Inside the water were these baby seahorses. That seemed really odd to me when I woke up. So, I described them. I said they were tiny, fragile, beautiful, bony, simple, delicate, expensive, alien and deep-dwelling. I realized that something in my waking life at the time matched that description. We were trying to start a family and I was exploring fertility treatments. I realized that the seahorses were representing my impression of an embryo. Once I made that connection, I was able to put the dream in context because I could substitute "embryos" into the storyline of the dream where seahorses had been.

#18 Notice Gender

Masculine energy is goal oriented and moves outward from the self toward others and into the world at large. It is active; it challenges us to go out and conquer.

Feminine energy is present minded and moves inward toward the self. It is passive; it challenges us to take stock of what we have directly available to us in this present moment.

These are just a few descriptors of masculine and feminine energy; there are many more. But for the purposes of our little dream resource here, this is enough to get you started. Consider the ways the gender of your dream characters could be symbolic of the movement of, or imbalance of, the masculine and feminine energy in your life.

Explore each character based on his or her gender qualities. How might the behavior of the men in your dreams express your masculine energy? Notice the women in your dreams. How are they representative of the way you use your feminine energy in life?

#19 Make an Image

Art engages the creative side of your brain, which is also, conveniently, where your dreams emerge. When making art, you're engaging both the unconscious dreaming mind and the conscious waking mind.

Dream imagery is ready-made for artwork. You'll find that as you try and decide what, exactly, to draw (or paint, collage, etc.), you'll learn more about which aspects of the dream are most important to you.

The colors you use, the size of each stroke you draw on the page, and the shape are all entirely up to you. The beauty of creating an image from your dream is that you'll be bringing it into form in the external world. Sometimes, when you do that, you will find that the dream has more to say to you. It will become an image you can return to again and again to consider its meaning.

As you work, notice what waking life associations crop up in your mind. Jot them down and reflect on them after your artwork is completed.

#20 Get Out of Your Head

Some of the best ideas often come to us when we least expect it. Brilliant, creative solutions pop up while we are in the shower or out for a walk. When it comes to dream work, you can employ the same technique of getting out of your head to bring about new "Aha!" connections.

First, think about the dream. Get the experience of it in your mind with as much detail as you can. Then, get up and do something physical. It can be anything so long as you're moving. Do this for as long as it takes for the dream to drift out of your thoughts. Once you've let your mind wander aimlessly for a bit (I find that it takes at least twenty minutes for me), return to the dream and start the mental exploration of it once again.

Getting physical will engage your body's wisdom. It will dislodge the dream from your conscious mind, letting it sink down into the depths where your inner voice resides.

#21 & #22 Join a Dream Group

A dream group is a gathering of people who are interested in discussing dreams and their meanings. There are dream groups all around the world. A simple internet search should turn up groups in your area.

There are two ways to work with your dreams using a dream group. The first (#21) is to simply attend a dream group. The second (#22) is to share your dream in a dream group.

Being in a dream group will give you a sense of community with other people who find dreams fascinating and who wish to discover the inner wisdom that can be found in their dreams.

I have participated in dream groups since 2007. Meeting in community to discuss dreams and the symbolic language of the dreaming mind is always educational, whether or not I share one of my own dreams. Simply listening to others discuss the symbolic language of dreams helps me in future interpretations.

If you attend a dream group on a regular basis, eventually you will have an opportunity to share your own dream with the group. This experience will provide you many new ideas to ponder concerning the meaning of your dream. Just like this book, group feedback adds to your collection of potential ideas to consider for your own interpretation.

The give and take of a group setting can be one of the most rewarding ways to work with your dreams.

#23 Incubate a Dream

The interesting thing about your dreaming mind is that, while you cannot control it, you can make suggestions and potentially influence it. Incubating a dream is one way to have an impact on what gets expressed at night.

Incubating a dream means setting an intention to dream about a specific topic. If you are stuck on a particular dream's meaning or on one aspect of a dream, you can ask your dreaming mind to try again.

Here's how to go about it. Review the dream you're struggling to understand. Get clear about where you want more insight. Maybe there is a particular character you want to know more about, or maybe there is a part of the dream that is fuzzy or hard to recall, for example. Then, as you begin to drift off to sleep, set a clear intention to gain more insight into that particular aspect of the dream.

You can repeat a question over and over as you fall asleep. Or, you can just say the intention out loud and let it go. Some people even choose to write their intention, question or desire down in their journal before turning out the light.

When you wake up, write down the very next dream you remember. Note: You may have to repeat the practice for a few nights before remembering a dream. That is normal. Just keep incubating a dream until you can recall one in the morning and write it down.

When you incubate a dream, take what you receive and work on the two dreams in tandem as if the second one is offering clarity for the first.

(#24) Tell the Dream in Present Tense

Most of the time we tell a dream in the past tense because it has already occurred. By shifting your perspective and viewing the dream as if it's happening in the present, you might remember new details you could not recall before.

Instead of, "I was in this building and the hallway was really dark. I was headed somewhere...."

Try saying, "I am in this building. The hallway is really dark. I don't know why it is dark. I am going somewhere...."

This is a slight shift in the way you recount the dream, but it can help you experience it more accurately or with greater detail. It might also give you new ways to explore the dream. In the example above, you can see a new detail has been added. When we began to explore inside the image of the dream as if it is happening now, we added the observation, "I don't know why it is dark." That detail is now part of the dream experience and can be explored as new information.

When a new detail about a dream comes to you, use it to compare to waking life. With our new detail, we can now look for waking life associations to the statement "I don't know why it is dark." You might then ask yourself, "Where in waking life do I feel like I am inexplicably in the dark?"

It is best to tell the dream in present tense in a way that you can capture and reflect back on the story of the dream, either by writing it out in present tense or telling the story of the dream to a witness who can listen closely for new observations.

#25 Focus on the Good Ones

One of the ways to work with your dreams is to look at the humor in them and delight in their capacity to remind you to lighten up.

Because dreams are drawn from our strong emotional content, they are oftentimes dark and serious. It's much easier to notice and pay attention to our dreams when they scare us awake. But if you only give them your time and energy when they scare you, then you might not work with your dreams very much. That leads to avoiding dream work and hoping you sleep through the night without remembering a dream.

But when our emotions spike in a positive direction, our dreaming mind can reflect that back to us in a wild, funny, and light-hearted way. Thank goodness for those dreams! If you work with the positive dreams, you'll open yourself up to inviting more dreams to stick around in your mind. Thus, giving you more dreams to work and helping you learn to trust that your dreaming mind is working on your behalf.

If you're going to work with your dreams, be sure and use some of your time and energy on the good ones. They may be reminding you about your strengths and progress. The good dreams help us remember to celebrate ourselves every now and then.

#26 Buddy Up

We all need a friend in this world, especially when it comes to telling our dreams. But, here's a not-so-secret fact: Not everyone wants to hear your dream. I mean, I do, but not everyone will.

Still, many of the dream strategies I've suggested in this book have to do with discussing the dream. So you're going to need someone out there to listen. You may even need him or her quite often if you're a prolific dreamer.

I was lucky because when I first became interested in working with dreams, my sister got into it with me. She and I would call each other up (sometimes daily) and swap dreams. Having her for a dream buddy was helpful, especially when I began uncovering surprising—and sometimes emotional—truths. The other benefit, besides psychological support, is that your buddy may point out surprising details or connections to waking life that you hadn't thought of yet. Two minds are better than one when it comes to dream work. Remember, though, that such brainstorming is just that; not everything offered by your buddy will resonate.

Having that partner will give you the confidence to stay on the path of dream work. Just be sure to listen to his or her dreams as well. As a bonus, you'll find working through symbols and connections for your friend's dreams will make you wiser when deciphering your own.

#27 Look for Opposites

We've established by now that I believe that your dreams are not random. I want to further point out that *nothing* in your dreams is random. Nothing. Your dreaming mind is very specific in its choices. If you are shown two things that are opposites in your dream, take note. Rather than representing two different things, it may really be representing one thing from two different perspectives.

Say, for example, that in a dream you are floating away from the ground. You look down and see a man digging a deep hole. *Floating away* and *digging down* are opposite actions; both moving away from the ground. Opposites, by nature of being opposites, are saying something beyond just the two things themselves; they represent the relationship between them. In this example, the two movements *away* and *down* are suggesting something about the ground that I was, presumably, standing on when the dream began.

By looking at dreams from this perspective, you move beyond the obvious elements and delve deeper into more of the subtleties that your inner voice regularly makes use of in dreams.

Other examples of opposites in a dream would be day and night or fire and water, adults and children, inside and outside, etc.

#28 Pray or Meditate

Dreams come to us out of our unconscious mind. They bubble up out of our own depths. Dreams are influenced by and entangled with all of our mental activity, our fantasies, our deepest desires and fears, and all of the clutter we take in within our lifetime.

The same can be said for prayer and meditation. Like dreams, they are also influenced by and entangled with all of our mental activity, our fantasies, our deepest desires and fears, and all of the clutter we take in within our lifetime.

They all exist in the same interior landscape, so it makes sense that they might all speak the same language, the language of symbolism and metaphor.

So one way to work with your dreams is to spend time in prayer or in meditation about the dream imagery. Holding the dream lightly in your mind as you meditate or pray might produce some deeper truth about the dream that you hadn't seen before. This is not just a fluffy, feel-good suggestion. Sitting with a dream image while also invoking your connection to the Divine and focusing in on the present moment will shift you into a new way of perceiving the dream images.

#29 Be More Specific

Describing dreams in greater detail will open new avenues for your reflection. For example, if you dream about a lake, that may tell you one thing. But if you describe the lake in more detail as *silver, cold,* and *exotic*, that adds a new dimension of expression to the symbol of "lake."

After describing the dream symbol in more detail you might ask yourself, "Does that combination of adjectives fit as an appropriate description of something in my waking life right now?" This sometimes works to jog your memory of something that you would describe in the same way as the dream symbol.

In our example, silver, cold, and exotic might just turn out to be the perfect description of the office building at a new job you recently started. That would give you the connection you need to understand that the dream has something to do with your new job. Then, you unpack the rest of the dream while considering what it might be trying to tell you about your new job situation.

Using your journal and sharing with a friend will help you capture the specific detail in your dreams with greater accuracy.

#30 Work with a Dream Professional

Many professionals specialize in utilizing a person's dreams to fuel reflective inner work. We are sometimes hidden behind different titles, such as therapist, psychologist, spiritual director, life coach, dream coach, intuitive, or Jungian analyst. All of these titles represent different professions, but they all can include dreams as a facet of the work.

Any dream professional should be able to listen to your dream and help you unpack the layers it contains. One word of caution though; if you come across a dream worker who tells you what your dream means outright, go find another dream professional. Y'all, no one can tell you what your dream means for you. Your dreams are *from* you and they are *for* you, meaning that only you can determine their meaning.

Working with a dream professional means getting guidance on the wisdom that may be being expressed by your dreams. Guidance is not the same as outright interpretation. Guidance should include someone setting up a safe space for you to tell the dream, riding any emotions that might arise from the telling, unpacking the dream, and wrestling with any insights that might bubble up to the surface during the exploration.

What we dream professionals do is accompany you on the journey as you unpack a dream for yourself, guiding you, asking questions, and delighting in the discovery.

#31 Act It Out

Performing a dream in waking life can lead to a powerful shift in understanding. Dreams happen in the privacy of your mind, but by performing the dream you bring the experience out of your mind and into the "real world" where it can be more easily reflected upon.

Most dreams are too full or complicated to act out in their entirety. I suggest that you have a person with you who can participate (with your direction) or simply bear witness to the dream story as you act it out. Having a witness gives you someone to discuss your ideas or realizations with as they surface.

Many books and movies are the result of a dream that was brought into the realm of waking life through the desire of the dreamer to share the experience with other people. Who knows? Maybe performing your dream will lead to a new epiphany for the next blockbuster.

#32 Let it Go

Sweet reader, you don't actually have to work your dreams. The truth is that dreams are working on your behalf whether or not you do anything with them.

What a relief to know that you don't have to catch a dream when it happens. While I do, of course, advocate strongly for doing dream work in your life, I also think it's important to keep it in perspective. Your dreams won't stop just because you don't focus on them.

One of the final suggestions I have for you if you can't seem to make heads or tails of a particular dream's messages is to just let it go. If you let go of a dream every once in a while, or even on a regular basis, it's okay.

Your dreaming mind is persistent and can send the same message in later dreams. If there is some wisdom in the dream that you're supposed to be getting, you can trust that you will hear it again in a future dream.

#33 Look for Movement of the Divine

One way to work with a dream is to ask the question, "Where is the movement of the Divine in this dream?" Rev. Robert L. Haden Jr., author of *Unopened Letters from God* and founder of the Haden Institute, taught me this powerful dream question.

It is a profoundly deep but simple question that can be applied to all dreams. In my opinion, it brings you quickly into the contemplative mindset of wonder and curiosity.

Unpacking a dream can feel superficial sometimes. We like to know that a red cardinal means new birth or that dreaming of flying means success in waking life. We like simple answers that point us in straightforward directions and lead to easy-to-follow adventures.

But asking yourself, "Where is the movement of the Divine in this dream?" can lead to more meaningful dialogue about your dream and might just set you on the pilgrimage of a lifetime. This question takes dream work to a deeper, more meaningful level and softens your perception so that you are able to see the deeper purposes at work in dreams.

A Final Word

I hope this collection inspires you to explore your dreams more deeply and to give your dreams a chance to share what they know with you.

Dreams proved to be a lifeline back to myself when I was lost in my own dark night of the soul during a particularly difficult chapter in my life. Maybe your dreams can bring you home, too.

If you are interested in more, you can find me at SweetGeorgiaPam.com and on social media as @SweetGeorgiaPam.

I am always interested in invitations to lead workshops, retreats, dream groups, lectures, and more, all around the country.

I enjoy hearing from people who, like me, are enamored with their dreams and who have come to see them as gifts of love from their very own depths. If you have a story to tell me about your work with this book, or if you have questions about dream work, please speak up. I would love to hear from you.

Pamela Muller

About the Author

Sweet Georgia Pam is a gifted dream expert and talented leader, director, and teacher who has been facilitating dream groups since 2007. She lives with her husband and son in Johns Creek, Georgia.

In 2005, Pam began an eight-year journey through infertility. This dark night of the soul led her away from teaching in a classroom and into an interior spiritual journey where she emerged changed, strengthened and ultimately serving others in a new, more deeply personal way.

Pam is blessed beyond measure and uses her joy to lift others up and help them look at their dreams as a source of inspiration to guide them through deep, reflective inner work.

She's been a featured dream expert on area radio stations and a presenter at such conferences as the Women and Spirituality Conference and the Summer Dream and Spirituality Conference.

Her training includes a bachelor's of science degree in education from the University of Georgia and a two-year training certificate for spiritual direction from the Haden Institute. In addition to facilitating dream group experiences, she also teaches workshops, meets with clients individually, and posts articles about dream work and spirituality.

Pamela Muller

Praise for Sweet Georgia Pam, from Clients and Colleagues

"Pam is incredibly gifted and intuitive."

"I was startled by Pam's accuracy. I have recommended her services to several friends and always rely on her when I have particularly significant dreams."

"Pam is open, flexible, respectful, and creative."

"Pam Muller is truly inspired and gifted!"

"Pam is a sweet and talented spiritual director who invites us all to look at dreams with a new, childlike curiosity and wonder."

"I will never be the same after this!"

"Trust me, you will adore her!"

Made in the USA
Columbia, SC
04 February 2023

11749432R00026